DRUNK-ONYMS

Duncan de Sorderly was born into the infamous de Sorderly brewing family in northern England. He now runs west London wine merchant, 'You Had Me at Merlot'. This is his first book.

DRUNK-ONYMS

128 WORDS FOR WHEN YOU'RE ABSOLUTELY TRASHED

DUNCAN DE SORDERLY

Illustrations by Josephine Dellow

HEADLINE

Copyright © Headline Publishing Group
Illustrations Copyright © Josephine Dellow

First published in 2024 by
HEADLINE PUBLISHING GROUP

1

Cataloguing in Publication Data is available from the British Library

Hardback ISBN: 978 1 0354 2644 7

Typeset by CC Book Production

Printed and bound in Great Britain by Clays Ltd, Elcograf S.p.A.

HEADLINE PUBLISHING GROUP
An Hachette UK Company
Carmelite House
50 Victoria Embankment
London EC4Y 0DZ

www.headline.co.uk
www.hachette.co.uk

DRUNK-ONYMS

Airlocked

- to drink so much you are deprived of oxygen

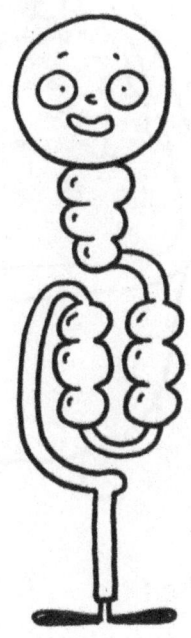

Ale-washed

- to be so drunk you might as well have bathed in ale

Annihilated

- to be so drunk you are figuratively dead

Arseholed

- to be so drunk you can't tell your elbow from your . . . yes

Banjaxed

- to be so drunk your body, mind and spirit are broken

Battered

- to be so drunk you possess the intellect of fried food

Bevvied

· to be so drunk you are completely empty
  of thought (except about your next
  drink)

Bingoed

- to be in such a state that you can't tell if there is one little duck or two

Bladdered

· to inflate yourself with alcohol

Blasted

· to be so drunk that you have no concept
of how loud you are (hint: very)

Blind

- to be so drunk that you cannot see

Blitzed

- to be so drunk that you may as well have put your brain in a blender

Blootered

· to be so drunk that balance
  is a thing of the past

Blotto

- · to be so drunk that your head is like a Lotto ball machine

Bombed

· to effectively destroy yourself with drink

Bottled

- to be so drunk you may as well get in the bottle you're drinking from

Buzzed

- to be so drunk your thoughts are replaced with white noise

Cabbaged

- to be so drunk that your brain is an actual vegetable

Canned

· to be so drunk you've preserved yourself

Clobbered

- to be so drunk it's as if you've almost been knocked out

Cocktailed

- to be drunker than expected due to the fact your drinks taste like sweeties

Cottled

- to be so drunk you have regressed to infancy and need to be put to bed

Floored

- to be so drunk you become one with the floor after spending so much time laying on it

Foggy

- to be so drunk your brain has developed
  an internal weather system. Warning:
  low visibility

Foxed

- to successfully appear less drunk than you actually are

Fried

- to have consumed so much
  alcohol it sends a shock (or
  two) to the system

Fuddled

- to be so drunk you can't tell which is
  your drink – perhaps all of them?

Gassed

- to be so drunk you're no longer solid, and simply float from one bar to the next

Gazeboed

- to be so drunk you possess a lower IQ than a glorified tent

Ginned

- to be drunk, specifically on mother's ruin

Gone

- to be so drunk that your personality is erased. Warning: alter egos may rear their heads

Groggy

- to be so drunk that to all intents and purposes, you are asleep

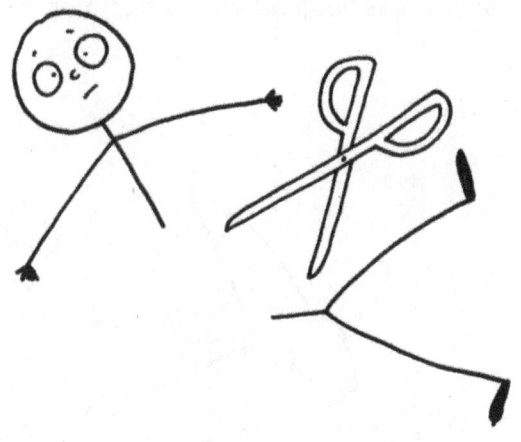

Half-cut

- to be so drunk that you no longer feel whole

Hammered

- to be so drunk that your head feels
  as if it has been hit with a hammer

Hooched-up

- to have drunk all the colours of the rainbow

Hosed

- to be so drunk you want to curl up outside in a dark corner

Inebriated

· to be incapacitated by drink

In his cups

- to be drunk in an old-fashioned, Jazz Age sort of way

Intoxicated

· to be so drunk you are toxic

Jazzed

- to be so drunk
  that you develop
  a heightened
  opinion of your
  musical ability
  (earplugs advised)

Jolly

· festively drunk

Juiced

- to have consumed a large amount of alcohol hidden beneath fruit juices

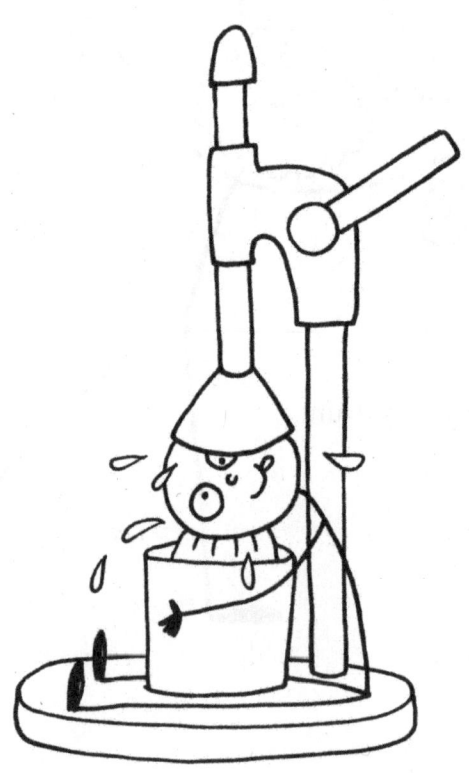

Lambed

- to be so drunk it is like your brain is made of wool

Lamped

· to be so drunk you see sparks flying

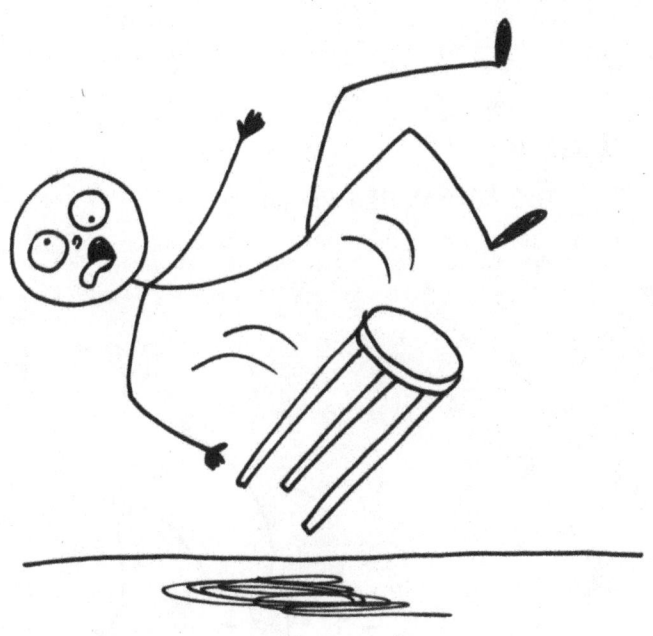

Langers

- to be so drunk you fall over, a lot

Lashed

· to be drunk like a cowboy

Leathered

- to be so drunk your skin has changed texture due to all the alcohol

Legless

- to be so drunk that you can no longer reliably control your limbs

Liquefied

- to be so drunk you're a puddle on the floor

Lit

- to be so drunk you're on fire
  (figuratively or otherwise)

Loaded

- to be so drunk your drinks are starting to feel like burdens

Locked

· to be so drunk you're trapped
  inside your own mind

Looped

- to be so drunk you keep doing and saying the same things over and over again

Lubricated

· to be so drunk everything just slips away

Mangled

- to be so drunk you're totally incoherent

Mashed

- to be so drunk you're no smarter than creamy potato

Mellow

- to be pleasantly drunk

Merry

· to be so drunk that climbing a Christmas
  tree seems sensible

Moppy

- to be so drunk your head feels like it
  has mopped up all the booze

Mortal

· to be so drunk you are suddenly
  conscious of your own limited time on
  this earth

Mullered

- to be so drunk you can no longer see straight

Nappy

- to be so drunk you are an infant version of you. Warning: a nappy may be required

Obfusticated

- to be so drunk that directions seem meaningless

Obliterated

· to be so drunk you have lost your sense
  of personhood

Oliver Twist

· to be drunk enough but
  convinced you want
  some more

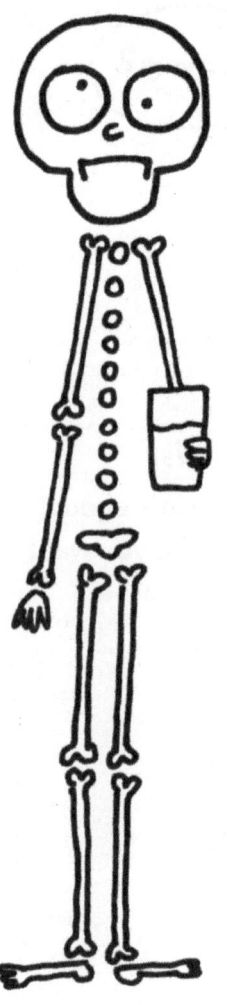

Ossified

- to be drunk to your bones

Overrefreshed

- to have carried on drinking past
  the point of no return

Paralytic

· to be so drunk you're no longer
  sure what is real

Pickled

- to be so drunk your blood has taken on the properties of preserving vinegar

Pie-eyed

· to be so drunk you can't focus

Pissed

- to be so drunk that public urination seems almost a civic duty

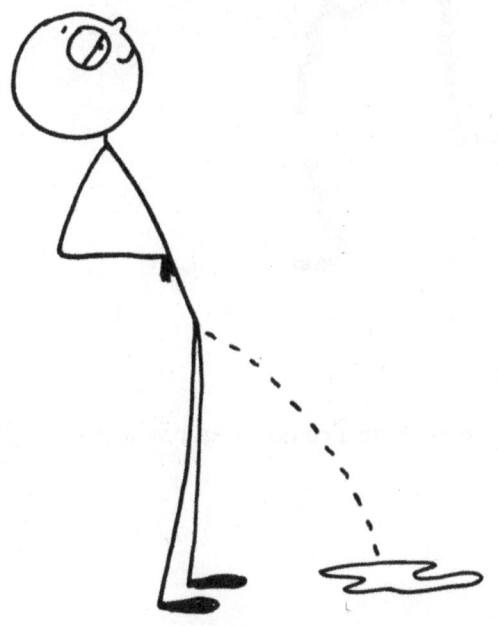

Pixilated

· to be so drunk you're no longer whole

Plastered

- to be so drunk you need to stick close to a wall for support

Plonked

- to be drunk on headache-inducing cheap wine

Polluted

- to be so drunk you're considered a contaminant

Potted

- to be so drunk you act no smarter than a little seed that's just been planted

Puggled

- to be so drunk a pug would beat you at Scrabble

Ramsquaddled

- · to be so drunk that sheep
  are your new squad

Rat-arsed

- to be so drunk you think all your
  ideas are genius (they're not)

Ratted

- to be so drunk a rat could outplay you at football

Razzled

- to be so drunk
  that you
  overestimate
  your own dancing
  abilities

Ripe

· to be just the right level of drunk
  for the night ahead

Rolling

- to be so drunk you feel like a pig in a blanket

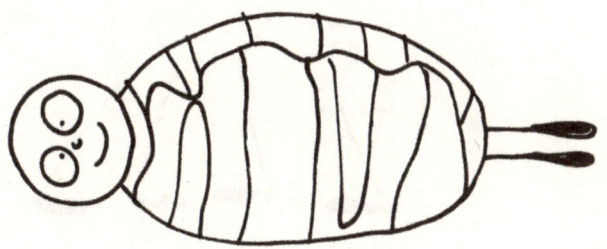

Rubbered

- to be so drunk you want to erase either yourself or the past few hours (or both)

Ruined

· to be so drunk you are
  internally collapsing

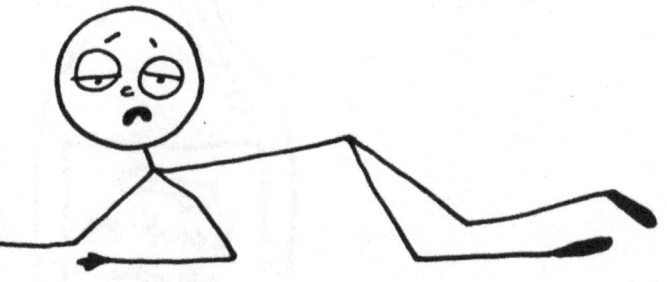

Sauced

· to be so drunk you are
  marinaded in alcohol

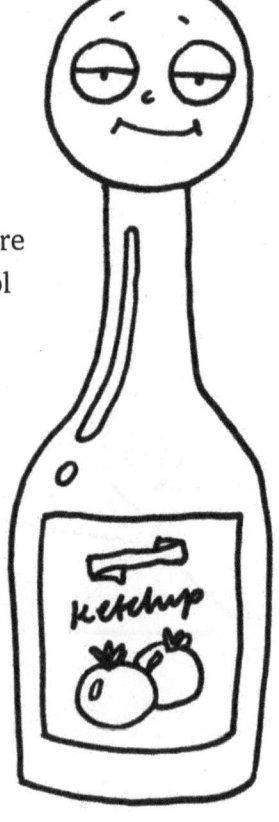

Screwed

- to be head-spinningly drunk

Shitfaced

· to be so drunk you may be hugging porcelain later

Skunked

- to embrace the psychoactive and olfactory properties of drink

Slammed

· to be flattened by drink

Slap-happy

- to be so drunk you can't feel pain
  (don't worry, you will later)

Slaughtered

· to be too drunk to be considered alive

Sloshed

- to be so drunk you find it hard to keep your drink inside your cup

Smashed

· to be broken by drink

Snookered

- · to be defeated by drink

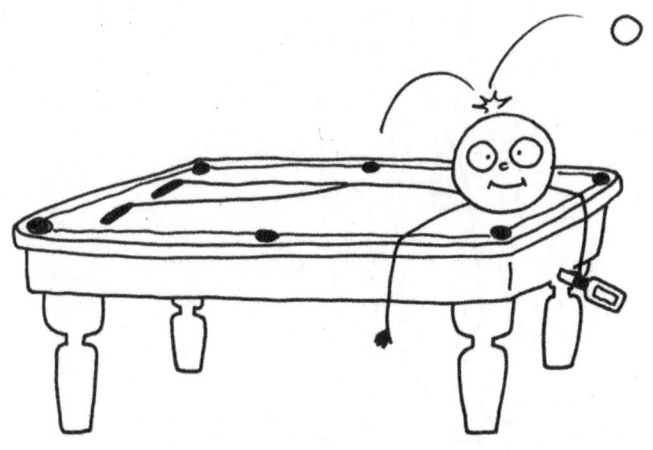

Soaked

- to be drunk all the way through to your centre

Sozzled

  · to be awash with alcohol

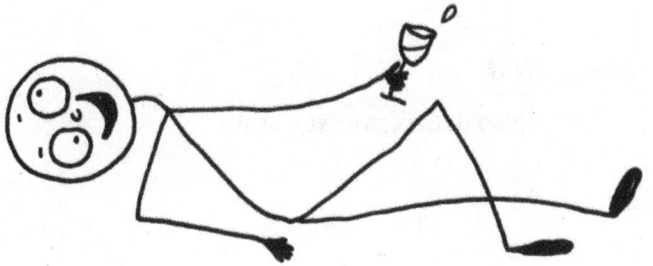

Spangled

· to be so drunk you see stars

Spannered

- to be so drunk that everyone thinks you're a tool

Squiffed

· to have a tipsy feeling of endless cheer

Steaming

- to be so drunk you are surrounded by a vapour of alcohol

Stewed

- to be so drunk the alcohol has infused with your very being

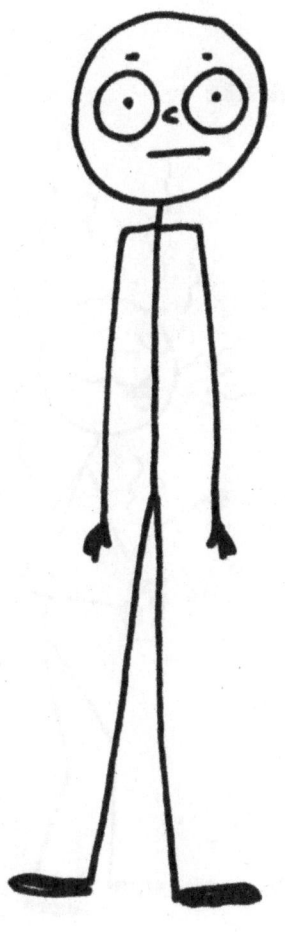

Stiff

· to be so drunk
  you can't move

Stinking

- to be so drunk you smell like a sticky pub carpet

Stoned

· to be tranquilised by drink

Stonkered

· to be emboldened by drink

Swamped

- to be so drunk you resemble (and possibly smell of) marshland

Tanked-up

- to have consumed enough alcohol to fill a fish tank

Three sheets to the wind

- to be so drunk that a light breeze would push you over

Tiddled

· to be daintily drunk

Tight

· to be constricted by drink

Tipsy

- to be picnic-perfect drunk

Toasted

- to be so drunk you're slightly warm and covered in crumbs

Trashed

- to be so drunk that you belong in a dustbin

Trolleyed

- to be so drunk you have the momentum of a shopping trolley on a hill

Trousered

· to be so drunk you pocket things
  that aren't yours

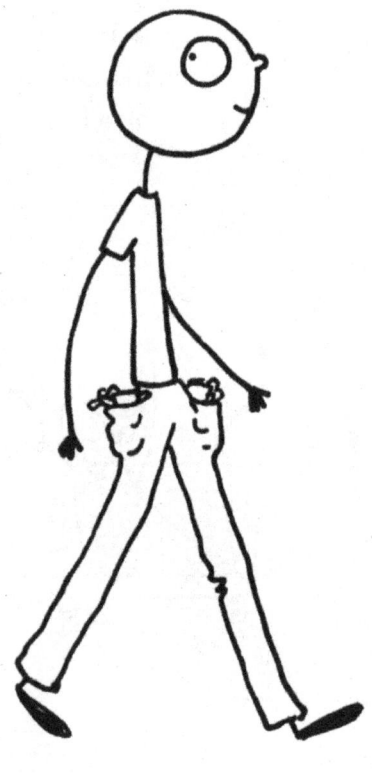

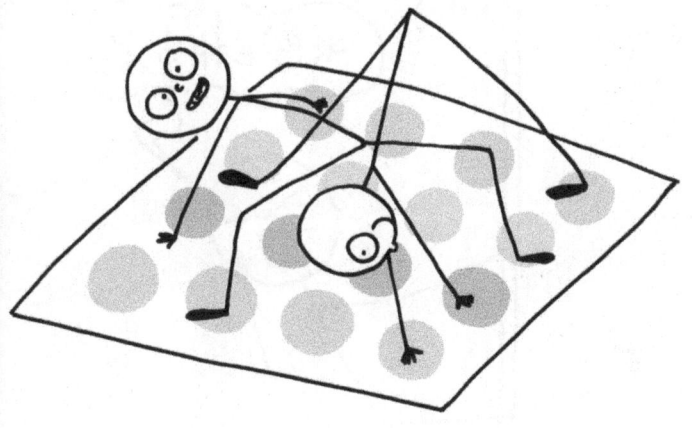

Twisted

- to be so drunk you no longer hold your normal shape

Wankered

· to be so drunk your
vocabulary mimics a
sailor's

Warped

- to be so drunk that shapes are distorted

Wasted

- to be so drunk that even the idea of a takeaway makes you feel ill

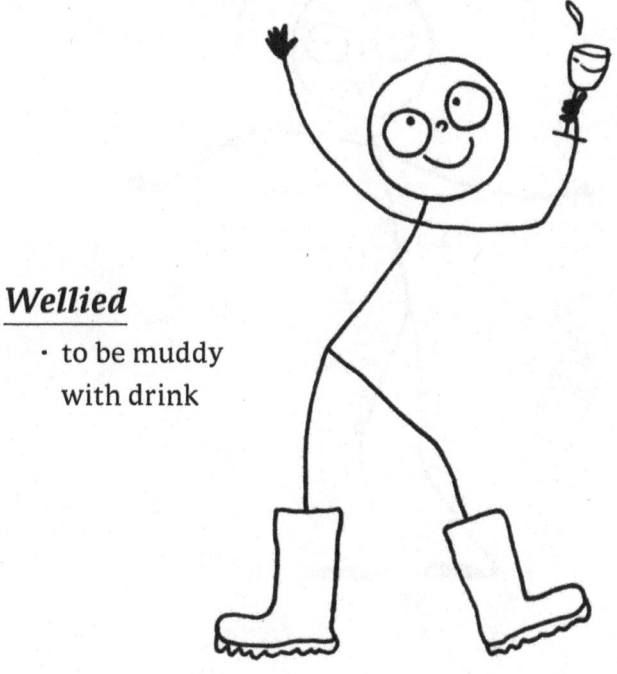

Wellied

- to be muddy
  with drink

Well-oiled

- to be socially lubricated by drink

Wiped

- to be so drunk just moving your drink to your mouth is exhausting

Withered

- to be so drunk that you look like a wilted flower, at best

Wobbly

- to have consumed so much alcohol
  you've lost your balance

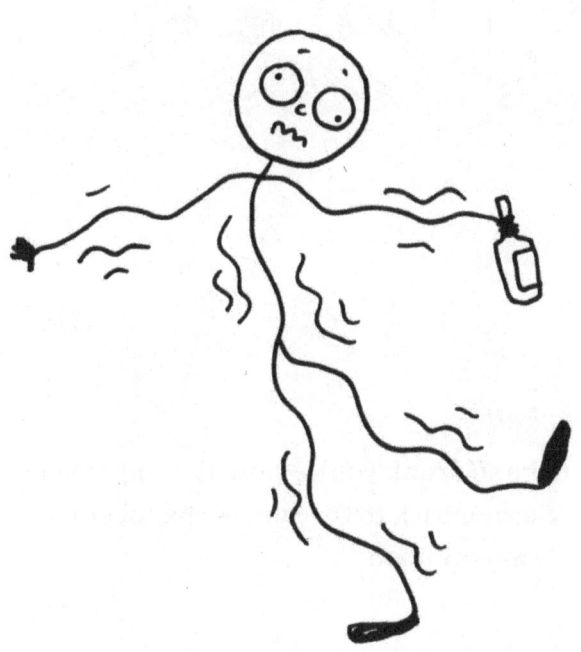

Wrecked

- to be so drunk you've sunk the ship that'd take you back to the land of the sober by tomorrow noon

Zombied

- · to be so drunk it's like your brain
  has been removed

Zonked

  · to be comatose with alcohol